Me

Henri Barbusse

(Editor: Henry Roujon)

(Translator: Frederic Taber Cooper)

Alpha Editions

This edition published in 2022

ISBN : 9789356894907

Design and Setting By
Alpha Editions
www.alphaedis.com
Email - info@alphaedis.com

Contents

INTRODUCTION

ONE day—it was neither in war time nor during manoeuvres—on a July morning, with the sun shining radiantly, a squadron of cuirassiers passed at full gallop across a magnificent field of ripening grain, in the neighbourhood of Poissy, although on every side there were wide reaches of fallow land and pasture.

When this hurricane of horses and men had, like a blazing meteor, devastated and laid low the splendid gold of the crops, two men remained behind, surveying the scene with visible satisfaction and undisguised interest.

One of the two was tall and the other short. The tall man was Colonel Dupressoir, who had directed the manoeuvre. The other, an elderly man, short of leg, and ruddy of complexion, with a long beard, white and silken, and a singularly expressive eye, was the painter, Meissonier. The latter had achieved his object. Thanks to long insistence and the payment of indemnities, he had brought about the passage of cavalry across that field, in order that he might make studies from nature, needed for a painting then in hand, *1807*, of how standing grain looks after it has been crushed and trampled by the onrush of a charge.

The whole artist, whose work we are about to study side by side with his life, is summed up in this anecdote. It reveals one of the most typical sides of his temperament, and, consequently, of his talent: a constant and scrupulous endeavour, maintained even at the price of sacrifices that would seem excessive to the layman, to interpret nature precisely as she is. It was this noble ambition—and we shall find other examples of it in the course of an artistic career in which it was the dominant note—that made him say to his pupils, with a conviction that commanded respect: “If I should sketch a horse from memory I should feel that I had been guilty of an insult to nature!”

PLATE II.—LES ORDONNANCES
(Tommy Thierry Collection, Musée du Louvre)

Every one of Meissonier's pictures is a document which may be profitably consulted if one wished to decide a detail of costume or armament. His consciousness in this regard has become proverbial.

And it is because he conceived his ideal after this fashion that this unerring painter of so many military types and scenes never attempted to picture skirmishes or battles. It was not that he did not want to, or had not cherished the dream of doing so. But he had never seen a battle; and a battle is a thing that cannot be reconstructed, like a marching column or a detail of camp life. Accordingly he painted none, because he decided, with a certain loftiness, *that he did not really know what a battle was*!

Let us keep this attitude of mind before us, and even underscore it in our memory. For this alone, in a vague way, would suffice to characterize the artist with whom we are concerned; and his whole long, rich, and fruitful career may be summed up as a successful and varied application of one great principle: devout and inflexible respect for reality.

EARLY YEARS

When Jean-Louis-Ernest Meissonier was born at Lyons in 1815, under the fading light of an Imperial sunset, these were scarcely the ideas that predominated in the national school of French art. Pictorial art, to confine ourselves to that, had, both before and during the First Empire, achieved at most a lumbering and trammelled flight; and the influence of antiquity, so perceptible in the language as well as in the manners and fashions at the close of the Eighteenth Century, served only to confine the inspiration of artists more strictly within the bounds of classic tradition. Roman characters, Roman costumes, Roman virtues,—such was the ideal to which each debutant who did not revolt openly must make surrender! To be sure, the commanding figure of David gave a magnificent prestige to this rather cold and dishearteningly classic programme. But, like all great artists, David was exceptional; and he stands today as the only one who, in an epoch sadly poor in genius, produced a host of living masterpieces, to swell the lists of a school so artificial that it would now be forgotten, save as an echo of his name. It is true that, by way of ransom, he spent much time in painting vast canvases that today hold but a small place in his life work.

On the threshold of the Nineteenth Century, in 1799, Eugène Delacroix was born. It was he who brought a new spirit into French painting and, single-handed, wrought a great revolution.

Such is not destined to be the rôle of Meissonier! His was neither so tragic a struggle, nor so immense a triumph. Unlike Delacroix, he did not restore the Beautiful nor hand down new forms to glory. He succeeded none the less in inscribing his name in modest yet precise characters—that will long remain legible—upon the marble of the temple.

How did the artist get his start? According to the monotonous and mournful formula, "after a hard struggle." The lives of all beloved and admired artists have this in common with fairy tales: they always begin badly and end happily (unluckily, they sometimes end a long time after the death of the principal hero!).

The father of Meissonier was a dealer in colonial products and chemicals, and kept a drug and provision shop in the Rue des Ecouffes. Beneath the low ceiling of this shop and between walls lined with drawers, bearing strange labels, the childhood of Jean-Louis-Ernest was passed. His mother was a fragile woman. We are told further that she was sensitive to music and that she had learned to paint on porcelain and to make miniatures.

Are we at liberty to attribute to the tender and brief contact of that mother, who died so young, with the life of her child, the origin of his artistic vocation? It is pleasant at least to fancy so and to try to believe it, even though we are told that parents bequeath to their children, not a vocation—a mysterious gift, of unknown origin—but rather a certain number of necessary aptitudes and qualities, which will enable them to profit by the gift, if perchance it falls to them from Heaven.

Yet the fact remains that in the depths of a cupboard, in the house on the Rue des Ecouffes, there lay the paint-box which Mme. Meissonier once used, while taking miniature lessons from the authoritative hands of Mme. Jacottot. As joyously as other children would have appropriated a jar of jam, the boy possessed himself of the magic box, and on that selfsame day entered, with stumbling fingers, upon the laborious mission which was destined to cease only with his life.

He was not a very good student. A report has been preserved of his standing in a school in the Rue des Francs-Bourgeois, at Paris, where his later childhood was passed. In this document the proper authorities alleged that the pupil, Ernest Meissonier, showed "too marked a tendency to draw sketches in his copy-books, instead of paying attention to his teachers."

The said tendency did not fail to awaken anxiety in M. Meissonier, the father. It should be remembered that, for some years previous, the question of painting in France had been taking on a rather bitter tone. The romantic school was entering boldly into the lists, and among its champions were some who distinguished themselves less by their works than by their long beards and the public challenge they flung at their traditional enemy, the phalanx of David's pupils. And among the latter, it must be owned, the majority made no answer beyond a disdainful silence and some mediocre paintings,—with just one single exception: the admirable, undoubted, impeccable exception of the great Jean-Dominique Ingres.

The press, the art clubs, not to mention the salons, were all more or less divided between the romantics and the classicists, the innovators and the traditionalists, and fanned the flames of a quarrel which, in view of the worth of the two leaders—one of whom spelled genius and the other perfection—was destined to appear without sanction to the eyes of posterity.

But, as may be imagined, these tumultuous polemics were not calculated to reassure a thoroughly pacific bourgeois, already much alarmed to find that he had begotten an artist. And just at this crisis another damnatory report exploded, this time from a master of the eighth form in a school on the Rue de Jouy: "Ernest has a decided talent for drawing. The mere sight of a picture often takes our attention from our serious duties." This diagnosis, so categoric underneath its familiar form and somewhat faulty grammar, sounded a serious cry of alarm. It was promptly heeded by the father, and young Ernest was forthwith entered as a druggist's apprentice, in a house on the Rue des Lombards.

Yet it was not long afterwards, thanks to a dogged persistence, that the lad had overcome paternal opposition and was allowed to do head studies in charcoal, at the studio of a certain Julien Petier, whose slender artistic fame rested solely upon the fact that, once upon a time, he won the *grand prix de Rome.*

Meissonier very shortly quitted this somewhat dull discipline, and he stayed scarcely longer in the studio of Léon Cogniet, which at that time was quite celebrated. Yet during the four months that he remained under the guidance of the worthy author of *The Four Seasons*, it must be admitted that he laboured greatly to the profit of his art.

M. Phillippe Burty, his contemporary and his first biographer, explains to us that, while at Cogniet's, young Meissonier did not work like the other students, from casts or nude models: "He passed his days in an enclosure adjoining the studio, where the master was engaged upon his ceiling painting for the Louvre, the *Expedition into Egypt*, and hired by the day soldiers in republican uniform, dragoons, artillerymen and their horses." In the midst of this resurrection of a past that was still quite recent, in the very presence of the stage setting, the reproduction of the Napoleonic Epic, he suddenly conceived of it as the greatest of all subjects that might tempt his accurate artist fingers. It must have seemed to him, later on, that he himself had witnessed its close.

PLATE III.—THE CONFIDENCE
(Chauchard Bequest, Musée du Louvre)

This painting, given to the Louvre in 1908 by M. Chauchard, is one of the most beautiful in that famous collection, owing to the incomparable naturalness of the attitudes, as well as to the finished art of its composition.

But while waiting to achieve his dream, he had to achieve a living. This was not easy. His father spared him an allowance of fifteen francs a month, not counting the privilege of dining at home once a week, and from time to time allowed himself to be cajoled into buying a small aquarelle.

Be one's tastes never so modest, it is difficult under such conditions to make both ends meet, and there was many a day of sacrifice and privation for the future painter of canvases destined later to sell at a hundred thousand francs per square decimeter. He shared his poverty light-heartedly with a chosen circle of friends whose fame in after years has made their names familiar: among others Daumier, the caricaturist, and Daubigny, the great landscape painter, with whom, it is told, Meissonier collaborated in manufacturing for the export trade canvases that were generously paid for at five francs a meter!

He was unable to enter the classes of Paul Delaroche, the monthly charge for admission to the studio from which *The Princes in the Tower* had issued reaching the exorbitant sum of twenty francs! He had to content himself with frequenting the Louvre.

Unlooked-for windfall: in company with his friend Trimolet, a needy artist who succumbed to poverty before his real talent had had time to ripen, he obtained an opportunity to decorate fans. Then, some religious figures and emblems of saints for certain publishers in the Rue Saint-Jacques. This meant the assurance of an honest living; they could go to a restaurant twice a day, every day in the week, and proudly pass the paint-shop knowing their account was paid.

When only sixteen years of age, Meissonier exhibited for the first time. As a matter of fact his name appears in the Salon catalogue of 1834, accredited with *A Visit to the Burgomaster.* In this picture one may find, I will not say *in miniature* (since all his paintings were destined to be contained in narrow limits) but in a youthful way, an indication of those qualities of relief and of realism which so energetically stamped his productions later on.

Is there any need of saying that the public failed to distinguish a work which did not sufficiently distinguish itself?

The first connoisseurs to pay attention to the newcomer were editors, the severe and imposing editors.

Not quite at the start, naturally; and the first instalment of illustrations that he offered to a magazine then famous, the name of which is now forgotten—four little sepia drawings—was curtly rejected. But he refused to be discouraged, and not long afterwards deliberately made his way to the celebrated art-publisher, Curmer. This bold venture went badly at the start. The publisher, rendered distrustful by so youthful and importunate a face, assured the young man and the friend who had introduced him, that "for the time being he had nothing for him."

But by a providential hazard, the short conversation which followed as a matter of civility before leave-taking touched upon the subject of life-masks. At that time life-masks happened to be quite the rage: people had their faces moulded in plaster just as nowadays they sit for a photograph; and young Meissonier related, not without vanity, that on the preceding Sunday he had taken the mask of the Johannot brothers, and he added that he knew those two princes of engraving quite intimately.

Famous acquaintances are always useful; the proof of this is that M. Curmer accepted an invitation to go the following Sunday to Meissonier's studio, to sit for his life-mask,—and, once there, it was impossible for him not to order an aquarelle.

The door of this publishing house, however, was as yet only half-way open to the artist; for when his friend Marville, "an etcher in soft-ground, mediocre but prolific," talked of having him collaborate on the Curmer edition of *Paul and Virginia*, the publisher, a prey once more to his original distrust, entrusted him to begin with,—with just one of the special illustrations,—to re-engrave!

Meissonier acquitted himself brilliantly of this half-task, with the result that he was entrusted with several other illustrations for the celebrated edition of *Paul and Virginia*, of which no bibliophile can ever speak without enthusiasm. But, on the other hand, he had an entire series to make for an edition, no less sumptuous, of *The Indian Cabin*, also a work of Bernardin de Saint-Pierre.

FIRST SUCCESS

And then, in the words of one of his contemporaries: "The first rays of fame that caressed him streamed from those admirable and diminutive drawings for *The Indian Cabin.* He had done much sketching in the Jardin des Plantes, in the conservatories, where the flora of the tropics expanded opulently; also, before the windows of those shops of bric-a-brac, abounding in exotic objects, which in those bygone days stretched in a row facing the entrance to the Louvre, on the Place du Carrousel. All that he had to do was to rummage among those sketches in order to give his composition an inimitable stamp of truth, such as was seldom attempted by illustrators of his nation. It was a simple thing to convert into an ornamental letter a storm-broken lily, a group of Indian weapons, some Javanese musical instruments. If the text called for the 'emblems of mental toil,' the young artist heaped his table with volumes bound in parchment or full calf, acquired for a few sous from the stands along the quays, and he had only to copy, with all the naïveté of the Primitives, the gleam of the edges, the bands on the backs, the slips of paper alternating with the silken bookmarks."

And the critic proceeds to cite an example of that "prodigious finish" which Théophile Gautier subsequently recognized as the most *popular* characteristic, so to speak, of his noble talent: "In two of these miniature vignettes, measuring less than four centimetres, two engravings can be made out, hanging upon a library wall; one of them interprets quite scrupulously *The Pariah thinking of the English Doctor*, and the other *The English Doctor thinking of the Pariah.* Between these engravings can be made out, hanging on a nail, and possessing all the characteristics described in the text, *the pipe of English leather, the mouthpiece of which was of yellow amber, and that of the Pariah, the stem of which was of bamboo and the bowl of terra-cotta.*"

The success of this *de luxe* edition was rapid and important. The first step along the path of glory was taken,—and on that path the first step costs more than anywhere else. Henceforth, no more need of soliciting work; far otherwise. The artist still continued to do illustrating. Mention must be made of the drawings that he did for *Frenchmen Painted by Themselves*, and later—here ends this chapter of his artistic career—the plates that served as illustrations for *The Fallen Angel*, by Lamartine (edition in two volumes, already unobtainable twenty years ago), and the *Contes Rémois*, by M. de Chevigné; this last series bears date 1858.

ETCHINGS

Let us add, for the sake of being complete, without wasting undue space upon side-issues, that Meissonier also experimented in etching. Authoritative critics assert that these attempts, in which the master modestly refused to see anything more than "essays," will eventually become "the most precious treasures that bear his signature."

PLATE IV.—1814
(Chauchard Bequest, Musée du Louvre)

This picture, so masterly and so dramatic in composition, is assuredly one of the most widely known in existence. The sombre visage of the Emperor, the severity of the landscape, the prevailing tone of sadness, admirably rendered, explain the wide favour enjoyed by this celebrated work, further popularized in engravings.

Besides, with one exception,—*The Smoker*, popularized by a large printing,—they are quite limited in number, and already eagerly sought after by collectors. And with all the more reason, because, at the fairly distant period of which we speak, the perfected processes for preserving the burined lines on the copper plate in all their original fineness and precision had not yet been invented; accordingly, the later proofs in his series of etchings betray a wearing of the copper which could not fail to lower their value. At the time of Meissonier's death, a proof of *The Preparations for the Duel*, in which the signature was legible, "in the lower left corner," brought upward of one thousand francs.

The most beautiful of all Meissonier's etchings are, without question: *The Violin*, which he engraved with a burin at once powerful, delicate and, as some critics phrase it, "vibrant," to adorn the visiting card of the celebrated lute player, Vuillaume; *The Signor Annibale*, representing, in braggadocio pose and costume, the celebrated actor, Régnier, of the Comédie-Française, in a rôle that is by no means the least celebrated in Augier's *Adventuress*; and *The Troopers*, seven figures whose personalities stand out rather curiously and exhibit a picturesque diversity.

The Reporting Sergeant was a miniature sketch made, in order to try the ground, on the margin of the plate on which *The Smoker* was etched. It is a finished and charming little work, full of expression, of life and actuality, condensed into a microscopic square of paper.

But what of his paintings? We left them for a time, in order to clear up certain points regarding Meissonier's incursion into the realm of the engraver,—an incursion from which he brought back, incidentally, both fame and fortune.

PAINTINGS

He profited from it above all in being able to continue to paint. For the fact remains that, from the time of his youngest efforts, such as *The Patrol Removing a Body from an Outpost*, his earliest known work, one of the collection that his father bought, to swell somewhat that famous monthly income of fifteen francs, he never abandoned his brushes.

We left him unsuccessfully exhibiting, at the Salon of 1834, a small painting, dealing with a Flemish subject. Let us add, as a final word, that this *genre* picture was accompanied by an aquarelle, entered in the catalogue of that date as: *Soldier to Whom in the Citizen's House, a Young Girl serves a Mug of Beer.* This aquarelle was purchased for one hundred francs by the Society of Friends of Art.

The following year he did not exhibit. This, unfortunately, was not because he had nothing to offer; but the pictures that he sent, consisting of *The Chess Players* and *The Little Messenger*, had not been accepted by the jury. There was an excess of severity in this refusal; and in spite of the fact that the candidate for admission was still under the age of twenty, the two pictures offered possessed certain genuine qualities that rendered the sentence of the jury cruelly unjust.

Such was the opinion of the artist, who in 1836 offered the same pictures over again; it was also the opinion of the jury of that year, for it accepted them.

Two years later, Meissonier exhibited a *Monk Consoling a Dying Man.* This canvas attracted the attention of the Duke of Orleans, who bought it for five hundred francs. (Fourteen years later, at the sale consequent upon the Duke's death, this same *Monk* was resold for 4,000 francs.)

In 1839, Meissonier attracted the attention of the critics. For example, you may find in a paper called *L'Artiste*, in a critique of the Salon: "And I almost forgot an adorable little *English Doctor*, by M. Meissonier, a charming miniature in oil, extraordinarily fine and subtle." These lines were signed by Jules Janin, who at that time maintained over French criticism a sort of sacerdotal sovereignty, comparable only to that which, so far as the national school of painting was concerned, was afterwards held by the artist whom Janin then heralded with an almost exaggerated cordiality.

PLATE V.—AWAITING
(In the Musée du Louvre)

This painting, which is frequently confused with another by the same artist, entitled *The Man at the Window*, is chiefly noteworthy for its finished detail and prodigious ability of execution. Meissonier herein reveals his profound understanding of the principles of chiaroscuro.

But the small size of Meissonier's pictures! That is the one thing that, for the world at large, contemporaries and posterity alike, is the keynote of his talent: "Meissonier has always painted on such a small scale!" That is what one would begin by saying, if one wanted to explain him, to reveal him to some one who did not know him. And what endless things have been said in addition, by way of praise, criticism, and discussion, regarding the scantiness of the canvases or panels to which the artist applied himself!

Underlying this whole matter of smallness there is, without any paradox, a rather big question. Beyond doubt, material dimensions in works of art are not taken into consideration, so long as these dimensions remain within moderation. It is equally certain that, short of introducing revolutionary modifications into our aesthetic creed, we would refuse to accept as a work of art anything that exceeded too far these limits of moderation, or fell too far below them. Is it not the same in life and in society, where exaggerated giants and undersized dwarfs find that they are outcasts, each in his own way, outside the common law, and regarded simply as curiosities?

Granted: but what is the limit? Does Meissonier surpass it, and are his pictures *too small*?

Very well, let us answer categorically: no! No, they are not too small, considering, first of all, their subject; secondly, their mode of presentment, their composition, their treatment as to decoration; and, lastly, the vividness and intensity of their details.

One may even go a step further and assert that they have the dimensions that they ought to have, the dimensions that are best calculated to enhance the artist's magnificent gifts, and to make one forget the qualities in which, perhaps, he was lacking. The scenes which he kindles into life, to say nothing of single characters that he portrays, are like stories told in an intimate sort of way; they force one to draw closer.

They have not sufficient harmony and amplitude to attract attention from a distance; but, seen from near by, they give their message with exquisite precision. They offer a hundred subtle details for us to seek out and approve; a painstaking grouping for us to admire; and, best of all, expressive physiognomies for us to read. It seems as though the dimensions had been calculated on exactly the right scale to awaken all these impressions at once and blend them as completely as possible. And all this would have been too scattered in an ampler setting. It is because of this perfect proportion that it has been so justly said that "Meissonier's pictures never look small excepting before you have really looked at them."

But let us make no mistake in this regard. Painting on a small scale would not of itself suffice to attain this maximum of intensity. It needed, on the contrary, an enormous amount of talent to avoid an effect of fussiness and preciosity.

Still other reasons have been given for the great value of this artist's works in spite of their smallness, or rather because of their smallness. M. Gustave Larroumet has written on this very point a brilliant and ingenious special plea, of which the following is the principal passage:

"There is a certain class of subjects in which amplitude is an error of judgment. If you wish to paint the coronation of Napoleon, the bridge of Tailebourg, or the battle of the Cimbri, you have the right to measure your canvas in proportion to the space which such scenes occupy in reality; on the other hand you might conceive of your subject in such fashion that it could be contained completely within a square metre. But why give to an artistic reproduction more relative importance than the originals have in reality? Supposing you wish to show me a passer-by, on foot or on horseback. How do they interest me in real life? Simply by the rapid impression that they leave upon my eye and mind. I have seen them at a distance, reduced to a few centimetres by perspective. I am satisfied if you show them to me in the same proportion."

The argument is specious. Perhaps it is more ingenious than it is well founded, and lays itself open to discussion. But it will not do to linger too long over abstract polemics, when we are in the presence of a reality, a type of work, every least portion of which makes its appeal and, by the very fact that it is so full of interest and of life, practically answers the subtle problem that it has raised.

In 1840 more pictures were sent to the Salon: a *Reader*, a *Saint Paul*, an *Isaiah*.

Was the painter beginning to change his manner? Those last two pictures might give reason to fear so. They were life size, yet that did not prevent them from being dull and commonplace in execution. Doubtless, irritated by his critics, Meissonier had wished to prove that he also, if he wanted to, could paint according to the schools. Even the artists who are surest of themselves sometimes come to these hasty and impatient determinations.

Fortunately for him, he made a bad showing, and a painter who had great influence over him, Jules Chenavard, succeeded in recalling him from the false path into which he was trying to force his talent.

On the other hand, the praises bestowed upon his *genre* painting, *The Reader*, which was "genuine Meissonier," could not fail to encourage him to remain true to himself. The *Revue des Deux Mondes*, in its critical review of the Salon, bestowed upon this picture an enthusiastic tribute, couched in a style that may seem to us today somewhat old-fashioned:

"A Flemish canvas, if there ever was one. Picture to yourself a good old soul, retired from business, his skin as wrinkled as the parchment of his books, ill clad, ill fed, and nevertheless the happiest man in the world: he is a bibliophile, and he is in the midst of old books! You could hardly believe how vividly this noble passion is expressed in that little picture. But where in the world did M. Meissonier come across all those delightful little rarities in books? You can almost smell the adorable odour of old bindings!"

The young artist—he was at that time only twenty-five—was awarded a third-class medal. The following year he obtained a second-class medal, and his painting, *The Game of Chess*, won him a brilliant triumph: it was purchased by M. Paul Périer. It was a material triumph not to be despised: the picture brought two thousand francs, which at that time was considerable. The moral triumph was even bigger, because Paul Périer was an experienced collector, who acquired only such works as were worthy to take their place in an assemblage where the biggest names of the period were represented by masterpieces.

Henceforth, success after success followed regularly. Each picture that he sent to the Salon won increasing distinction: *A Smoker* (they are a goodly number, the smokers and the readers that came from Meissonier's brush!); *A Young Man Playing the 'Cello; The Painter in his Studio*; *The Guard-House*; *The Young Man Looking at Sketches*; *The Game of Piquet*; *The Park at Saint-Cloud.* This last picture was done in collaboration; Meissonier painted only the figures, the landscape was the work of Français.

This mounting success, which so quickly turned into glory, was legitimate. The artist had by this time all his resources admirably at command, and was fully imbued with his ideal.

He had learned to give to every face that profundity, to every scene that intensity of action, that constitutes his individual bigness. The arrangement of the *milieu*, the scrupulous devotion to realism that we noted in the opening lines of this study, the prodigious anxiety to give to every one of his personages such play of physiognomy, such expression, glance, and gesture as would best reveal their character and help us to know them better,—all these things combine and harmonize to produce an effect of remarkable power.

PLATE VI.—THE PLAYERS AT BOWLS
(In the Casa-Riera Collection)

This curious composition represents some Spanish soldiers playing bowls outside the city wall. The painting, which is hardly larger than the accompanying reproduction, is a little masterpiece of actuality, and the people in it move in a thoroughly faithful landscape, lit by the warm sunlight of Spain.

Those among Meissonier's contemporaries who had assured taste and artistic insight were impressed by the number of qualities revealed in such limited space. Let us listen to Théophile Gautier:

"Meissonier," he wrote in an article published in the *Gazette des Beaux-Arts*, "composes his pictures with a science unknown to the Flemish masters to whom he is compared. Take, for example, a Smoker! The manner in which he is placed in the centre of the picture, one elbow resting on the table, one leg crossed over the other, one hand hanging idly by his side, his body sunk within his gaping waistcoat, his head bowed forward in revery, or jovially thrown backward,—all this forms a composition which, while not so apparent to the eye as some dramatic scene, nevertheless works its effect upon the spectator. The accessories cleverly play their part to throw more light upon the character of the central figure. Here is a Smoker, for instance, who is a worthy man, no doubt of it; clad in an ample coat of ancient cut, and of a modest gray, with a well brushed cocked hat upon his head; one foot swings free, encased in a good, stout shoe, with silver buckle; and, with the tranquillity of an honest conscience, he draws in a deep breath of tobacco smoke, which he allows to escape again in little clouds, wishing, thrifty man that he is, to make the pleasure last. Close at hand, upon a table with spiral legs, he has placed side by side a flagon and a pewter-lidded tankard of beer. An intimate satisfaction radiates from his face, which is furrowed by deep lines, a face expressive of foresight, orderly habits, and rigid probity. One could trust him with one's cash-box and account books. Here is another Smoker, clad in red; he also holds a pipe and performs apparently the same action; but his disordered garments, violently rumpled, buttoned askew, his three-cornered hat jammed down upon his eyebrows, his cuffs and frilled shirt crumpled by nervous fingers, his whole attitude expressive of feverish anxiety, his twitching lip straining around the clay stem of his pipe, his hand thrust angrily into an empty pocket,—all these details proclaim the adventurer or the gambler in hard luck. He is evidently saying to himself: 'Where the deuce could I borrow a louis or even a crown?' Even the background, if we consult it, gives further enlightenment. In this case we no longer have neat plastering of modest gray and substantial brown woodwork, but battered and dirty walls stained with smoke and grease, reeking of tap-room foulness and unclean lodgings. And that shows how far one smoker may fall short of resembling another!"

It is precisely this difference between one human being and another, in other words, this quality of individuality, that constitutes the creative gift of the real artist and proves that the honour of this title is really deserved by a painter whose pictures are animated groups, among whom a spectator may wander, studying them with growing interest, and then afterwards call to mind the various types, episodes, scenes, dramas that he has actually *seen.*

One can never grow tired of quoting Gautier apropos of an artist whose brush always had something in common with his pen. This masterly art critic has described for us, sketched in words, so to speak, still another picture: "A man standing before a window through which the daylight streams flecking his face with silver; in his hand he holds a book which absorbs his entire attention,—this is not a complicated theme, but it grips us like life itself. We want to know the contents of that volume, it seems as though we could almost conjecture it. Plenty of other artists have painted marquises and marchionesses, sleek abbés and shameless beauties of the Eighteenth Century, thanks to the aid of powder and patches and paint, rosettes, paniers, bespangled coats, silken stockings, red-heeled shoes, fans, screens, cameos, crackled porcelain, bonbonnières and other futilities. Meissonier rediscovered the decent folk of that period, which was not made up exclusively of mighty lords and fallen women, and of which we get, through Chardin, a glimpse on its honest, settled bourgeois side. Meissonier introduces us into modest interiors, with woodwork of sober gray, furniture without gilding, the homes of worthy folk, simple and substantial, who read and smoke and work, look over prints and etchings, or copy them, or chat sociably, with elbows on table, separated only by a bottle brought out from behind the faggots."

And who can ever forget, in *The Confidence* (the picture which passed from the gallery of M. Chauchard to that of the Louvre), how tense and attentive the face of the listener is, even in repose, while the relaxation of the body is revealed by his posture, as he leans against the wall with an elbow on the table,—and how naïve the face of his friend—younger and better looking—as he reads the letter: naïve, excited, even somewhat simple, with a nose slightly exceeding the average length and a forehead just a trifle too low.

In the *Game of Cards*, a soldier and a civilian are seated opposite each other, in the midst of a contest. The soldier has a dogged air and he is losing. Apparently, he is not a strong adversary, for the man of questionable age who faces him, his small, narrow, foxy head surmounted by a three-cornered hat, his lean body lost in the depths of a huge greatcoat, his thin ankle showing beneath the white stocking, belongs to the race of weaklings who live at the expense of the strong.

In *The Etcher*, just as in *The Man at the Window*—two of his most celebrated pictures (the former brought 272,000 francs, even during Meissonier's lifetime)—the interest of the principal—and only—figure is heightened and singularly beautified by a delicate effect of light, forming an aureole, in the very centre of the picture, respectively around the face of the worker and of the dreamer.

Note, in *A Song*, the moist eye of the musketeer playing the guitar, and in *Pascuale* the half stupid, half poetic air of the central figure engaged in the same occupation; note also in *The Alms-giving* the frowning brow of the horseman as he searches in his pocket; and in *The Visit to the Chateau*—an ostentation of coaches and gentry—and in *The Inn*—three cavaliers who have halted for the moment and are grouped around the serving-maid, as they drink—the reconstruction of an entire epoch with its pomps and its idylls, that justifies us in calling these pictures veritable "stage settings taken from life."

One might spend a long time in analyzing the various shades in the gamut of expressions on the faces of the principal and secondary figures in the *Game of Piquet*, who, scattered all nine of them around the two sides of the tavern table, follow either amusedly or critically or with feverish interest the changing fortunes of the game. And in the *Portrait of the Sergeant*, what a magnificent collection of different degrees of attention: that of the portrait painter as he studies his model standing in front of him on the pavement, in his finest uniform and his finest pose; that of the model intent only upon doing nothing to disturb his ultra-martial bearing, his gaze menacing, staring, fixed; that of the spectators, some of them drawing near, fascinated, another who casts an amused glance at the picture as he passes by, with some sarcastic remark on his lips; another who no doubt has just been looking, and for the moment, with pipe between his teeth, is thinking of something else as he sits on a bench with his back to the wall and his legs extended in front of him.

The Quarrel, with all the feverish violence that drives the two bravos at each other's throats, has perhaps more amplitude and less realism than any of the previously mentioned works. It is Meissonier's one romantic painting, and he professed a great admiration for it, ranking it as one of his four best canvases. It is recorded that the master said one day to a friend:

PLATE VII.—AMATEURS OF PAINTINGS
(In the Musée du Louvre)

This picture, which must not be confused with the *Amateurs of Paintings*, in the Musée Cluny at Chantilly, is nevertheless a replica of the latter. They are differentiated by a few insignificant details, but they resemble each other in the harmony of the grouping and the truth of the attitudes.

"I have seen my *Quarrel* at Secretan's. I looked at it as though I had never seen the picture before. Well, do you know, it is really a fine thing!"

MILITARY PAINTINGS

Mention should be made, before passing on to the military paintings, of just a few other genre paintings: *The Reading at Diderot's*, *The Amateurs*, *The Flute Players*.

But it is the military pictures that loom up largely amongst the artist's prolific output:—*1807*, the portrayal of the Imperial Apotheosis, the army passing by at a gallop, eagerly acclaiming the Emperor, as he answers with a salute; *1814*, the decline, the retreat from Russia; *1815*, the cuirassiers of Waterloo before the charge. This picture, which formed part of the Duc d'Aumale's collection, was purchased for 250,000 francs, but afterwards twice resold: the first time for 275,000 francs, the second for 400,000 francs.

Yet it may be said that the artist fully earned what some of these military paintings brought him. Although he mounted successively all the rungs of official honours (he was made Knight of the Legion of Honour at the age of thirty, Officer at forty-one, Commander at fifty-two, received the grand golden medal at the Exposition Universelle of 1855, and became a member of the Academy of Fine Arts in 1861), Meissonier nevertheless always led a singularly active and industrious life. Not only did he paint a prodigious number of pictures (in 1886, four hundred were already catalogued), but he took part in the Italian campaign of 1859 and in the Franco-Prussian war!

In 1859 he was, at his own request, attached to the Imperial Staff of the French army, dreaming, as he had himself acknowledged, of becoming "the Van der Meulen" of the campaign. At all events, he got out of it one of his best canvases: *Napoleon III. at Solférino*, which never left the Musée du Luxembourg until it was transferred to the Musée du Louvre.

He himself has related, with a delightful sense of humour, the machiavelian intrigues to which he resorted in order to secure the Emperor's consent to pose. For the idea of painting a figure, and especially the central figure, without a sitting, was a heresy that he could not even contemplate. Let us hear his own account:

"Would Napoleon III. pose for Solférino? That was what weighed on my mind most of all. You know my love for exactitude. I had revisited Solférino, in order to get the landscape and the battle-field direct from nature. You can understand how essential it was for me to have the Emperor give me a sitting, if only for five minutes. I managed things, I think, rather cleverly. I began by blocking in my picture roughly; then I invited an officer whom I happened to know, to come and give me his advice on certain military details. This officer, as I was aware, had served at Solférino. I led him on to tell the part he had played in the combat, and when the iron was hot I proposed that he should let me include him among the figures in my picture. He consented eagerly. When the portrait was successfully finished, he talked of it to other officers, who came to see it and, in their turn, offered to serve me as models. One of them was acquainted with Maréchal Magnan, and it was he who brought me Fleury, who in his turn brought me Leboeuf.

"The latter undertook to show my painting to the Emperor, and to that end secured me an invitation to go to Fontainebleau. Napoleon III. received me cordially, and after spending a long time in studying my picture, in which only one figure was now lacking, he inquired who, according to my idea, that missing figure should be. 'Why, you, Sire.' 'Then you are going to paint my portrait?' he remarked. 'How will you do that?' 'From memory, and with the help of published documents.' 'But all that is not equal to a single sitting,' replied the Emperor. 'Do you not agree with me, M. Meissonier?' 'Undoubtedly, Sire, but—' 'Very well, nothing is simpler, let us both mount our horses, and go for a short ride, and while we chat, you can study me at your leisure.'

"Overjoyed at the opportunity afforded, I rapidly formed a most mephistophelian plot. As it happened, it was precisely at Fontainebleau that my old friend Jadin had his studio. I manoeuvred to guide our course in the direction of that studio, and when we were at his very door, I boldly proposed to the Emperor that we should pay a visit to the good Jadin. He laughingly consented, and thereupon the two of us descended upon Jadin who, unprepared for either of us, was in his painter's blouse, smoking his pipe. The Emperor, greatly amused by this adventure, refused to let Jadin disturb himself. He rolled a cigarette and, taking his seat astride of a chair, entered into conversation. Meanwhile I had seized the first pencil that came to hand, and fell to sketching. The unforeseen sitting lasted for a good half-hour. It served me not only for the completion of Solférino, but for another picture besides, a little panel."

A fine example of artistic perseverance and diplomacy,—greatly aided, it must be admitted, by the complaisance of the interested Emperor.

Eleven years later—the year of terror—the artist, in spite of his fifty-six years, undertook active service. Yielding, however, to the entreaties of his friends, he left the army near Sedan, the night before the battle of Borny, and set forth alone, on horseback. His journey back to Paris was a veritable Odyssey. Along the road to Verdun he was constantly taken for a spy and halted. At Etain, he was taken prisoner, and owed his release solely to the universal renown of his name. It took him three days to reach Poissy, where he had his country home; and once there, he organized a national guard. But at the news of the investment of Paris, Meissonier hastened to make his way into the besieged capital.

The morning after the Fourth of September, he besought the Minister of War, Léon Gambetta, for an appointment as prefect in one of the departments that were either invaded or menaced. His patriotism was only partly satisfied; he was appointed Colonel in the staff of the National Guard. "The populace of Paris," says a witness, "when they saw that little man with florid face and long gray beard, and legs encased in tight leathern breeches, passing back and forth along the boulevards, often cheered him, mistaking him for the major-general of artillery."

The painter planned to commemorate the defence of Paris in a picture of colossal size. The project never got beyond the stage of an outline sketch, of deep and tragic interest.

Have we cause to regret this? Meissonier was an allegorical painter, and nowhere more than in his military pictures—both scenes and types—do his powerful and delicate qualities of penetrating observation reveal themselves. Every one of his soldiers,—trooper, musketeer, French guard, Grenadier of the guard,—in full uniform or in fatigue, or even in the disarray of the barrack-room, has his own personal physiognomy, and manner and temperament; they one and all *live*, and in them lives the conscientious and brilliant artist who laboured so faithfully to create them and succeeded so well.

Is it not because of this expressive relief both of figures and gestures that people were able to compare Meissonier to Marmot, and to say that "Meissonier was worthy to paint the stories of Marmot, and Marmot worthy to furnish stories to Meissonier"?

It would be only just, before leaving him, to defend the artist—who after enjoying a vogue that was perhaps a trifle too enthusiastic, has fallen, quite unjustly into slight disfavour—from two criticisms that have frequently been passed upon him. Too much stress has been laid on his lack of the gift of colour and the gift of grace.

PLATE VIII.—NAPOLEON III. AT SOLFÉRINO
(Tommy Thierry Bequest, Musée du Louvre)

Under any other hand than Meissonier's, the group constituting the Imperial Staff would have been banale in the extreme, but thanks to an ability that has no parallel outside of the great Flemish painters, the artist has succeeded in making these miniature figures veritable portraits of the shining military lights of that period.

To be sure, he is not a colourist in the grand, resplendent sense in which the word is associated with the names of Titian or Paolo Veronese; but it has been said with a good deal of reason, that he had a colour sense "suited to his range of vision." In view of the realistic and palpable clearness with which he saw things, he must needs adapt a soberly exact scheme of colour; for in any one of his works the dazzling and magnificent orgies indulged in by lyric poets of the palette would have been as out of place as a character from Shakespeare would be in the midst of a prosaic scene in our modern literal-minded drama. The colourists use their tints to paint dreams, transposing into a resplendent and intense register the tranquil harmony of the actual colours; they produce something different from what the rest of the world sees; something more, if you choose, but at any rate something different. The impeccable truthfulness of a Meissonier stubbornly adheres to that modest harmony which the others leave behind them in a soaring flight that sometimes verges on folly. One might prefer to have had him totally different; but, granting the serious forethought in his choice of subject and conception of structure, his colouring could not have been different from what it was.

As to his lack of charm and grace, that is a reproach which for the most part he took little trouble to avoid, for he hardly ever painted women; but it was a reproach which he in no way deserved when he did transfer them to his canvases. We need to offer no further proof of this than his adorable studies of Mme. Sabatier and the portrait that he made of her. The strange attraction of that beautiful face, so full of intelligence and fascination, the delicate and matchless suppleness of posture, all blend together in a compelling yet mysterious radiance with which only a great artist could illuminate his paper or his canvas.

Accordingly one should guard against any judgment too absolute, too definitely peremptory regarding a talent so rich in resources; but undeniably Meissonier greatly preferred to paint musketeers or grenadiers, to say nothing of horses.

Horses, by the way, were one of Meissonier's weaknesses. He owned some beautiful ones, and used them not only as models but also for riding. He spoke on many occasions of the incomparable pleasure that he found in directing "those admirable machines," which he defined as "the stupidest of all intelligent animals." But that in no way detracted from their beauty of form. "What a pleasure it is to make their mechanism work!" he confided to one of his distinguished friends. "Just think that the slightest movement of the rider, the slightest motion of hand or leg, the slightest displacement of the body have their immediate effect upon the horse's movements, and that a true horseman plays upon his mount as a musician plays upon his instrument. For the painter a horse is a whole gamut of lights and of colours. Its eye, now calm and now excited, the quivers of its coat and undulations that run through it, the variety of its lines and the infinite beauty of their combinations afford material for a whole lifetime of study."

And here again we meet, as in everything that he said and thought, that same love of detail, that meticulous admiration for reality and that cult of patient labour which is the secret of all that he achieved.

Furthermore, there was no moment in his remarkable career—which was destined to be crowned by an apotheosis when the artists of the entire world united in choosing him as president of the Exposition Universelle des Beaux-Arts in 1889—there was no moment in his career when he sacrificed the sacred principle of exactitude and of documentation which were the foundation of his splendid honesty.

Of this artistic virtue there are abundant examples. We have already cited one in the opening pages; we will cite another by way of conclusion: one of his friends called upon Meissonier at Poissy: "The concierge told me," this friend relates, "'Meissonier is in the studio opening on the court.' I found my way into that huge studio cumbered with sketches of every sort, with studies of horses modelled in wax and standing on pedestals. I waited a while, and then in trying to discover where a beam of vivid light found its way in through some crack in a door, I discovered, in the little court adjoining the châlet, Meissonier out in the blazing sunlight astride of a bench that did duty for a horse; heavy boots, breeches of white cashmere, uniform of grenadier of the Imperial guard, decorations on his breast, and, last of all, the 'gray redingote.' He was seated on a saddle lent to him by the son of Prince Jerome. In his hand he held a tablet on which was fastened a sheet of white paper, and he was carefully sketching himself, studying his reflection in a mirror. It was the middle of summer and the heat was atrocious. 'My model can't pose as Napoleon,' he told me, 'but I have exactly Napoleon's legs.'"

Is it necessary to say after this that no painter ever informed himself with such religious zeal in regard to costumes and accessories? Of the heroic Imperial Epoch which he worshipped above all others, he sought and gathered together all sorts of relics: not content with the possession of a white horse closely resembling that of Napoleon I., he used to point with pride, both in his collection and in his paintings, to a complete set of trappings that had once served the Emperor; and one of the greatest rages that he ever felt in his life was produced by the respectful but firm refusal of the Beaux-Arts to lend him the "Gray Redingote."

His "working library," as he called it, contained incomparable riches. It included breeches, hats, helmets, boots, shoes, pumps, buckles, walking-sticks, and jewelry. He would have been able, by rummaging there, to clothe from top to toe whole generations of bourgeoise, nobles, and labourers, from any epoch of French history, to say nothing of the various regiments and the staff officers! He quite literally bought out the stock of second-hand dealers in the Temple market, which up to the middle of the nineteeth century was the sales place of old clothes once worn by our great-grandparents and their ancestors.

And we know,—his fine passion for the truth was always cropping out,—that he actually suffered because he could not clothe his models with genuine old linen. At the end of some very conscientious researches that he had pursued in the Imperial Library, he considered that he had made a discovery that was useful to his art, when he read in the *Encyclopedia* that in the eighteenth century linen was cut on the bias, and not straight across, as it is today. We must not smile! For herein lay the secret of greater suppleness in the folds.

And when, detail by detail, his documentation had been completed, what endless sketches, experiments, rough drafts had to follow! For a single painting he acknowledged that he had to make whole "cubic metres" of preliminary studies.

In spite of all this, when the picture was finished and more than finished, it did not always please him. The same friend whose personal testimony we have already cited, informs us that one day, in his presence, the artist violently slashed up a painting which everybody else had pronounced perfect, while at that very moment a purchaser was waiting for it in the vestibule: "I don't know how to paint!" cried the artist in despair, "I shall never learn my craft."

There we have an impulse and a sacrifice which few painters would be capable of making in sincerity, and which define better than the longest dissertations could do, the soul of Meissonier, his talent and his glory.

CPSIA information can be obtained
at www.ICGtesting.com
Printed in the USA
LVHW041022020323
740706LV00008B/1133

9 789356 894907